Let's 'GO'!

Get Over To
Get On With Life

Let's 'GO'!

Get Over To
Get On With Life

Shalonda "Treasure" Williams

Tru
Treasure

A TruTreasure Publication
through

LOVEWALK
MOTIVATION SERVICES

Printing and Binding by
Createspace.com

Published by
TruTreasure Publications

through

Love Walk Motivation Services

Let's 'GO'!
Get Over To Get On With Life

www.treasurespeaker.co.cc
www.lwmotivations.co.cc.

If you don't bother the past,
the past won't bother you.
It's only an illusion.
Leave it where it is and 'GO' forward.

— Shalonda "Treasure" Williams

Acknowledgments

To my Great Creator and Source of Life, I acknowledge you. I acknowledge your divine presence within me and I thank you for the wisdom that you allow to flow through me. I pray that you continue to speak, write, motivate, encourage and inspire through me.

To Nicole A. Jones, also known as Nikki, I am grateful to you for your endless support. You titled yourself my number one supporter & fan and you have yet to fail in that stance. Thank you for believing in me and my endless dreams.

To Tauzhanae, Jerome, Andreas and Romell, I am ever so grateful for your existence. You are a great inspiration to your mother rather you think so or not. Thank you for loving me without any conditions. It helps me to grow; it gives me an example of how to pattern myself.

To my awesome editor and friend, Belinda Beck. To some we may make an odd pair of friends but I love you and I am grateful for your honestly, encouragement and timely evaluations. Thank you for receiving me just as I am and allowing my voice to still shine through. You believe in that voice and I am glad that The Creator allowed me to make your acquaintance.

To My Mommy, Mr. Tee, Big Sam, Rev. J. D., Grand Ma Marie, Ms. Agnes, Mother Wines, April, Melanie, Tanisha, Leah, Roman, Sam, Evelyn, TruSum, Marina, Damien, David, Rebecca and Cocco.

To the memory of Grandma Eva Mae, my sister Tammy, My beautiful cousin Octavia, Uncle Lucius, Aunt Eloise and to the man that made the best shrimp and rice and shark meat I ever did taste, my dear friend, Mr. Clarence Lynard.

To all of you that support without hesitation, I am grateful.

To all those have inspired me and motivated me from afar, be it through books, quotes, audio, songs or television. Thank you for walking in your divine purpose so that I could be inspired to do all that I am purposed to do. Oprah, congratulations on 25 years of your show which was a great part of your destiny and purpose. Because you follow your heart, so many were impacted. I look forward to seeing you in your next phase in life.

This book is dedicated to Samuel Springsteen Sr. (1947 -)
& Clarence Lynard (1951 – 2010).
Two gentlemen that have played awesome roles in my life.
This is to their bravery in fighting the disease known to
the world as cancer. I am awed by the strength and
courage it takes to keep smiling through it all.

Contents

Introduction

The ties that bind us are sometimes so strong that we can not seem to break free on our own. There are tons of circumstances, which we can all recall, that would make us feel justified in staying in our stunted positions. Emotional, physical, and mental anguish from our pasts have our hands and feet gripped and we are going in circles fighting to be free.

Imagine, you have just spent the past hour going on and on and on about the breakup. *It* hurt you so badly you feel that you are losing your mind. Your heart is aching and you can't stop crying. All you want to do is crawl up into a ball in the middle of your bed and just rock back and forth until the hurt all goes away.

Say you find yourself venting to a fellow co-worker about how hard it is to work for "those people". The hours are long, the work never ends and you haven't been able to take a break all day. The next day you come to work only to be asked to the office. You are laid off. Then you spend three weeks talking about how they didn't appreciate you, how you can't believe they would do that to you.

How about the fact that you tense up every time someone comes near you. What they did to you 20 years or 30 years ago is still etched so clearly on the tablet of your soul. Someone says to you, "Can I take you to lunch?" "No, what for? I've got nothing to give you." Or, "Can I take your jacket?" "I can put up my own jacket. I don't need anybody to help me." Talk about scarred! Then you complain to your friends and family that there are no good men or women out there any more, how you've been hurt one too many times and everybody is the same.

How about when you change your appearance based on what everyone else thinks is best, and then you talk about how people won't allow you to be yourself or just let you live your own life.

Then, there was the abuse and molestation. You were so young and you felt that no one would believe you so you kept it yourself praying that somehow their stench would just go away, that the image would just disappear from your mind's eye. To this very day, you still haven't talked about it. It hurts too bad to even think about telling.

All these things, whether they seem like big issues or minor issues, they are still the things that hold us captive in our hearts and minds. Some things we feel are worth talking about and some things we would rather bury deep inside. Either way it seems to seep out in some way or another. Mainly in our words, opinions and how we choose to live our lives.

Anger, hostility, depression, suicide attempts, low self-perception, promiscuity, vicarious living, underachieving and even, overachieving.

Most times we go on and on about this thing or that thing and how bad they are. Then comes the sobering, deliberate words of a friend or loved one. They look you straight in your eyes and say, "Just get over it." Yes! The words sting like bees on your neck. They hurt because you wanted someone to join your pity party and to be on your side. You wanted them to tell you that you were right, that you were justified in your feelings and that the whole world is wrong. But, they do just the opposite. They love you enough to say, "Just get over it."

Today, I am that friend and loved one here to offer you the same loving and heart felt advice. I am here to lift you to the 'GO' position. The position that says that it is time to 'GO'; "Get Over" in order to "Get On" with your life.

"Get Over" what? "Get Over" everything that has caused your growth in life, love, peace and faith to be stunted. "Get Over" the ties that have bound you and made you feel that your life is not worth living. "Get Over" the things that make you feel unworthy to be loved and that you will never amount to anything.

"Get Over" it all. Whether it be circumstances, nay sayers, haters, abusers, illness or your own decisions. It is time to get over all those things and begin to see clearly to a better, more abundant life.

In this book, you will be offered some realities that so many people had to deal with in order to feel peace in their lives right now. You will do exercises that I have applied to my life. You will learn a few things about how I lived through obstacles just to take steps toward my Divinely planned purpose. Yes, even I had to go through some things and come to some truths about myself!

I do not want you to take my "get over it" as you would take it from your nonchalant friend who couldn't give two cents about what you are going on about. Do not even take it as you would from your old associate who has his or her own bitterness to handle.

Take these words as you would from somebody's Nana or Big Mama who just fixed you a slice of cake and a cup of hot cocoa. She sits down across from you, turns your face to meet hers and says, "Baby, life is what it is. Things happen, but you are going to be alright. You have got to get over this so that you can get on with your life."

That's me for the duration of this work. Nana Treasure, sitting at the table with you, eating cake and drinking cocoa! I'm talking to you and telling you to "Let's 'GO'!"

Let's Get Over!

Get Over "The Cruels"

<><><><><><>

"It seems hurtful words hurt a little more when they spring forth from the mouths of the ones you love."

Growing up as a child you couldn't escape them. They were like meals at the Klumps, you were sure to get a good helping of them. They would never fail to find their way to your hearing, and they hurt like mad. What were they? Negative words. Hurtful words. Words that cut so deep that they made their way into your blood stream. These words were spoken by people who we will call "The Cruels".

Your parents may have started it all. They talked down to you as if you were such a disappointment to them. *"You will never amount to anything worth while."* If you were trying to behave, you were called a goody two shoes or either you were said to be up to something. *"You think you're slick. I know that you're up to no good. You are no good. That's what no good people do, no good."*

21

You decided to act out because they said that you were "too good". You wanted to give them a reason to look at you, to talk to you – even if they were screaming. However, you were punished and cursed out because you became the "problem child." You tried not to care, but the words hurt. Well, at least they gave you the attention, right? You tried with all your being to make them proud so that they could one day speak one positive statement into your ear. Nothing you did was good enough. But, you loved them and you wanted them to be proud of you. You tried everything.

Nothing seemed to work. To those parents of yours you were just not good enough and they never failed to tell you that. They reminded you of your "failures" so much that you began to believe that you were worthless and that you would never amount to anything.

Was it your single mother who made it her business to remind you that you looked and acted just like your "no good" daddy? Was it your father who told you that because your mother was into the "street" lifestyle that you were going to turn out the same way? Was it both parents who never planned for you and because they were not getting along it was your fault?

Maybe it wasn't your parents. Maybe it was your "so called" friends, your school peers, your uncle or your jealous cousins. What if it was everyone, all the time. Day in and out, "The Cruels" would find you. The words came from them so frequently that if they didn't, you began to think that no one remembered you were there.

<><><><><>

"I know about the effect that one negative person can have on your psyche and your self image."
- Willie Jolley*

Negative words have slain many hopes and dreams. Though, as a child, you used to dream all the time, as you grew, you stopped dreaming completely. You were told that dreams do not come true, and even if dreams did come true for some, they wouldn't for you. You were told you were worthless and that your dreams were stupid. "The Cruels" tell you that you don't have what it takes to accomplish anything big and you hear the lie, take it in and allow it to grow within you. *"They're right. I'm not good enough to do this. I can't go to that school. I can't be a doctor."*

You have gone from hearing the negative words to experiencing negative results. Instead of seeing each experience as a lesson, you take them as a confirmation that you will never succeed. You try out for the cheer-leading squad but you are not chosen. All you can see are the faces of everyone who told you that you have no chance of making it.

The negative words of others, especially people that you love, can have a profound effect on an individual. One of the hardest things to take is to hear how much of a mistake you are and how your loved ones think that you will never amount to anything.

The traumatic effects of experiencing "The Cruels" are very real and can cause of lifetime of self-esteem issues if you do not deal with them. Now! You have to be able to admit that the things they said were cruel and that it hurt you. *That* is dealing with it. However, you do not have to get down on yourself and stay in the place where negative words are the only thing you can hear. Their negative, cruel words should no longer matter. You must step into a new zone in, this, your life.

<><><><><>

"Let the cruel ones carry their own baggage. You are only carrying your own positivity from now on."

This is the moment when I am going to encourage you to 'GO'. It is time for you to wade in different waters. If you did not believe that there was even a twinkling of hope you would not be reading this book.

I know that deep down inside you want to get past all those words that keep ringing in your head. Those words that have flourished into beliefs. Beliefs that your size makes you ugly. The beliefs that your learning ability defines whether you will be successful. The belief that you will never be good enough. The belief that no one will ever love you. These beliefs are destructive and those that spoke them were more than likely victims of similar treatment.

Let's 'GO'!

It is now time for you to replace the old, destructive beliefs with new thoughts and beliefs. Leave it all in the past. Now is the time to 'GO'. Time to get over what "The Cruels" have said and walk in your new life of positivity.

Replace the old thoughts and beliefs that you have adopted as your own truth with new ones. How? The same way that the old ones were sown. You are going participate in what may seem like a battle. In some ways it may very well be. This battle will end in the defeat of your old, destructive beliefs.

You are going to begin by identifying what those old beliefs are that have been binding you up and making you fearful to truly live. You are going to take the first step in recognizing that the cruel words hurt you, however, you are ready to let it all go. Your present is happening now. Your future should not have to suffer, it has not even made your acquaintance yet. You can no longer let your present and your future pay the bill that your past ran up.

When you are replacing the old, you must state the new in a positive way. No future tense references. For example, "I AM a beautiful being. "I HAVE what it takes to achieve my goals." "I ACCOMPLISH all I set out to do." Now, "Let's 'GO'!"

Time To 'GO'!

What are the old, destructive beliefs that you have allowed to penetrate your mind? (List the ones that you remember.)

_____
_____
_____
_____
_____
_____
_____
_____
_____
_____

In what ways have these beliefs stagnated your life?

_____
_____
_____
_____
_____
_____
_____
_____
_____
_____

Take those old, destructive beliefs and replace them with new beliefs stated as my statements in the above content. Follow the rules. (No negative talk, only positive, do not say "I am going to..." It's I am or I have. No future tense.)

_____

_____

_____

_____

_____

_____

_____

_____

_____

_____

_____

_____

_____

_____

_____

_____

Get Over The "NayAholics"

<><><><><>

"There are people in this world who are so negative that I would say that they are addicted to the negative, addicted to saying nay. They are what I call 'NayAholics' ."

People who eat, sleep and breathe negativity. Thy are cousins of "The Cruels". As a matter of fact, they are related by the blood-type N: Negativity. They are so addicted to the negative that I have decided to call them NayAholics. It is their very own life language.

These are the people that can never find a positive side to the number line. Their vision is set to look left of the zero. To them, the right of the zero does not exist.

I have known a few "NayAholics" in my life. Those that I have encountered on my walk all had negativity as a base, however the motives behind their nays were each a little different. How is that possible? "They are all the same; always having something to say about everything."

Yeah, I get it. Just allow me to explain.

<><><><><>

"Unfortunately, sometimes it is the people who are in our inner circle and who really love us. They are not trying to be mean-spirited or discouraging, but they just have ' Possibility Blindness.' "
- Willie Jolley*

The first group of "NayAholics" say nay and actually believe that they have your best interest at heart. Most times, these people have seen a great deal of negative outcomes. The are set on not seeing you make the same "mistakes" and ending up just like "so and so". "You better not do that or else you're going to end up just like Pete. You know, he went out for that football team, got picked and then ended up with a broken ankle. You better not. It's too dangerous."

They honestly do not mean to discourage you. They do not realize that their fear of something bad happening is crippling them from living, and as a result is handing that fear over to you. They do not understand that one failed love affair does not mean that every love experience will end. Just because their parents marriage broke up, it is not set in stone that *yours* will too.

"You know, my mama and daddy didn't make it, every

man is a cheat. Once daddy cheated, mama should have known that he would do it again. That's why I don't waste my time, and you shouldn't waste your time either. That boy is just going to get what he wants and leave you at home with a boat load of children, and go on to the next one. Watch what I tell you."

It is what they have witnessed that causes this group of "NayAholics" to generalize every situation. The intentions seem good to them, yet you are now wondering why they always have something negative to say, why they say no or *nay*, to everything you want in life.

<><><><><>

"There is nothing worse than a friend who is not a friend at all and doesn't know it. They are afraid of being left behind or left out, so they devalue you with words because of their own insecurities."

Did you ever have a friend who was always telling you that you can't? "You can't save that much money. I tried it and it didn't work for me so you can't do it either." "I tried to get on with that company and they wouldn't hire me, so you might as well not even apply. If they didn't call me back they probably won't hire you either. I think they're prejudiced."

These "NayAholics" are the "I'm-out-so-you-gotta-be-

31

out-too people". They often believe that if they can't accomplish something, then no one else can accomplish it. This is actually a pretty big ego talking here. It is more than likely an unconscious form of arrogance on their parts. There are also times when it is just plain old, "*I'm better than you. They won't possibly see you as being better than me.*"

This person is the friend that has always done all they could to capture all the attention. They wanted to be the one out front so they chose you, the quiet best friend that no one took a second look at. It was easy to talk down to you because you had low self-esteem anyway. They even blamed you when something did not turn out in their favor.

It was never hard for them to talk you out of letting go of a brilliant idea because to you, their words were golden. "You can't wear that. Red looks bad on us." You can't! You can't! You can't!... because I can't.

Most times, these are the people who need to be negative to you so that you will never see your true potential. You would be surprised how much they actually envy you because they actually see the greatness in you that you may not. So, if they fail they will criticize you to take the spotlight off of themselves. This is their ego booster.

<><><><><>

"Weak people, nonleaders, and those who suffer failure and frustration as adults, repeatedly condemn, complain about, and criticize other people." - Brian Tracy*

"You will never be able to accomplish that. You're not smart enough. That job requires a lot more than what you have to offer," says the "NayAholics" known as the Dream Killer.

Dream Killers are among us. This group of people won't ever accomplish their goals, so they intentionally do not want you to reach yours. The difference between this group and the last is that it is not an arrogant ego speaking. It is a flat-out, HATER ego speaking. A "Hater" is slang for someone who is always talking down to someone, telling them what they can't do, or someone that is very jealous of what another person has or is in the process of getting and they want to kill it. They don't want to see someone have or get "it" because they never had it or plan to go get "it". This group actually has no intention of doing better. You do!

Dream Killers tell you that you should forget about your dreams because they are impossible. In actuality, they are just upset because something they tried failed and they are angry. They have not yet come to understand that just because an attempt did not go as planned, it does not mean that the entire plan has failed. They did not want to get up and try again because it hurt too bad. It hurts even worse to see you succeed.

<><><><><>

"Different test, same results!"

The motives behind the different types of "NayAholics" may be different but the results are the same. Blood-type N is in their body and it will only go away if they undergo a very important transfusion. They will have to replace that negative blood with positive blood.

The thing is, you do not have to be contaminated by these people. Some of them have been negative for so long that even when you try to speak positive words to them, they toot up their nose and call you crazy. If that's where they want to remain then it is not up to you to change them, neither is it your life sentence.

"It is okay to free yourself from anything that has a grip on you."

You are not going to stay under the spell of the "NayAholics". They have chosen their path, now you must chose yours. Do you actually believe that you can't? Do you want to walk around fearful that nothing will ever work? Do you want to stay back to babysit your best friend's ego? NO!

The answer is no. You are to answer no to all those questions. Your answer is simple. "I want to live a positive life and my mind is made up." Right?

Okay, it is your decision to make but I believe in you. I believe in your abilities and I say that you should go for it. I am not talking about walking around being mean to everyone who says something negative. No! I am talking about putting positive in and pushing negative out. This is your job. Though the task may seem tedious, it is doable. Let's 'GO'!

Time To 'GO'!

Name all the "NayAholics" in your life.

_____
_____
_____
_____
_____
_____
_____
_____
_____
_____

Identify the *intended* motive of each.

_____
_____
_____
_____
_____
_____
_____
_____
_____
_____

Now is the time to separate yourself from any and all

negative words. If the "NayAholic" is someone very close and you don't want to end the relationship, then you must make it known that you will no longer listen to any negative feedback. When they begin with the negativity, you will either leave or hang up the telephone. Be assertive, but not rude. Stay consistent. This is about *your* peace of mind.

From now on, when you hear someone say what you can't do, remind them that YOU CAN! Get by yourself, then began to repeat over and over that all things are possible. Say it until you believe it. Smile at yourself and thank the Source of Life that you have what it takes.

Also, do not share your dreams and hopes with "NayAholics". You already know what they will say. Until your positive attitude rubs off on them, only share your dreams with Dream Builders.

Get Over Self Defeating Thoughts & Habits

<> <> <> <> <>

"There was one person, a former teacher, who interrupted the years of negativity and low expectations for me by saying, 'Never let someone else's opinion of you become your reality.' "
- Les Brown*

"Nobody likes me." "I'll never get that promotion as long as Arthur is with this company." "I don't know why I auditioned for that part. I won't get it anyway."

Yes, we live in a world with "The Cruels" and The "NayAholics" and the words they speak are very hurtful and/or damaging to your ego. However, these people are not your worst enemies. They are just other Beings that have not yet learned to deal with themselves.

It is not their fault that you failed to try out for the dance, swimming or softball team. It was not because they

39

said, "You aren't good enough!" It's not because they were cruel to you that you did not want to speak up for yourself. No, they are not your biggest criticizer neither are they the ones keeping you from reaching your goals or going after your dreams. Your worst enemy is you. It is all about you.

<><><><><>

"But they... is not a legitimate reason to be stagnant."

But they were so hard on me. But they were so mean to me. But they told me I couldn't and I was so young... blah, blah, blah.

These are examples of some of the thoughts or words coming from someone reading this book. *But they...* is just what led up to the choices that ultimately rest with *you.* That's right. It was not the fact that someone told you that you were not good enough that kept you from going after the thing you wanted. It was your fear that they were right that kept you from going after it.

Dreams abandoned. Goals not completed. These are signs that you have lost sight of yourself and what matters. *But they...* It no longer matters what they have said or done. What matters now is where you will go and what you will attempt. Are you ready to get past the old lies and step up to the plate and take a swing?

But they... has now turned into your own self-defeating thoughts, and those self-defeating thoughts have led to self-defeating habits. Those thoughts and habits that have crippled you and that have kept you from truly dreaming, truly living.

<>< >< >< >< >

"A change in your thought lives will help you to see clearly and clear vision is required in order to see your great purpose." *

Self-defeating thoughts are when you tell yourself that you can't. It is you saying to yourself, "I'm not good enough for this job," or "I don't have the guts to start that business." The things you talk yourself out of have been so great that *you* have become the "NayAholic".

What are some of those self-defeating thoughts that have you stuck at the beginning of the movie? Well, we know that we can never get to the middle or the end of a movie if we don't press play or if the disc has finger prints on it. It is time to *clean* your mind; wipe off the smudges from your many past happenings. It is time to get over everything that has stopped you from going forward.

We are now dealing with you and how the issues from the past have led to your fearful thoughts. You have, up until today, been defeated before even beginning a task.

41

The reason is because you have been feeding your mind with constant negative, internal conversation.

Les Brown, in his book *Live Your Dreams,* says, "You may not always able to control what life puts in your path, but I believe you can always control who you are." This is so very true. Even though things have happened in the past, it does not mean that you have to allow those things to dictate the rest of your life. This means, changing those self-defeating thoughts that were planted by others, to self-assuring thoughts that will define who you are today and also give you courage to remain in that state of mind.

We are no longer going to allow self-defeating thoughts such as, "I won't ever be good enough", "I should just give up now", "Nobody will ever wants me" and "I don't have what it takes to make it", to clog our minds and leave us to live a negative life with no dreams being fulfilled and no goals being obtained. From this day forward we are going to change our thoughts. No more self-defeating. Only self-assuring.

<><><><><>

"The enemy within you weighs you down before the enemy that you fear on the outside can even get a chance to."

There are things that we do every day that confirm we live with self-defeating habits. These things come in all

42

shapes and forms and are very clearly.

One of the biggest self-defeating habits in the world is worrying. Though some may not know or understand that worry is a habit, it definitely is. Case in point, every time you see a bill in your mailbox you are already worried and concerned about how it will be paid before you even open it. There are also those who feel that this kind of worry is normal and that it is acceptable.

This statement is not true. Worry is never acceptable. One of the things that we must do in changing our self-defeating habits is to make sure that our belief in ourselves and in our Maker are intact. Whether you believe in God, a higher power, the universe or whatever you choose to call the divine power of the world, you must begin to believe and know that everything you need will be provided and that you are worthy to receive every bit of that provision.

Another self-defeating habit that is very common is the habit of talking down to yourself. This happens when those self-defeating thoughts are spoken out in words. When you tell yourself that you might as well not even try, you are telling yourself that you are not good enough for the thing that you are trying to accomplish. You are speaking out negative thoughts.

When you speak the negative words you are thinking you given the universe permission to use them. The fact that you spoke them means that you believe them. After today, after reading this chapter, you will begin to change this self-defeating habit by replacing it.

Just like self-defeating thoughts, self-defeating habits will cause a big pause in your life. You cannot go forward with anything that has the word self defeating attached to it.

<><><><><>

"Forward is the way to go."

How can you get past those self-defeating thoughts and habits that have caused your life to remain on pause for so long? If you are tired of the negative flow that has been happening in your life now is the time to make a change. That change begins with you. This step is not about anyone else but you. No matter what someone else on the outside does or says, you are responsible for your life's goals from this point forward.

There are those people who have suffered an extreme amount of trauma, abuse, drama and negativity. I have seen situations where people have laid down and stayed there. But, there have been others who have inspired me by the way they did not allow circumstances and situations to keep them lying on their backs. You can get up. You can start over. As long as you are breathing, every day is a new opportunity to start fresh. According to Willie Jolley, *It Only Takes A Minute To Change Your Life*. So, if it only takes a minute to change your life, imagine what you can do with the rest of the minutes in the day.

Your fresh start today is going to require you to, on purpose, replace those old self-defeating thoughts and habits with new, positive ones.

Time To 'GO'!

Unlike the exercise you did in the first chapter, you will not be trying to remember every self-defeating thought, you will simply began this exercise by speaking positive to yourself, intentionally, everyday and night.

What I want you to think about however, are some positive statements that may or may not feel comfortable to you at first. Such as, "I am qualified to do this job."

Below, I want you to write down as many positive statements as *you* can come up with. Do not look in any book or on any website. This exercise is all about you. By doing this on your own, you prove to yourself that *You Can*! You have the power, begin using it. I dare you to believe in yourself. I do!

_____

_____

_____

_____

_____

_____

_____

_____

_____

_____

46

Get Over "I'm Not Worthy"

<><><><><>

*"In order for your worthiness to actually count
for something, you have to realize it."*

What is your self-worth? It is respect for or a favorable opinion of yourself. Your worth as a person, as perceived by you. Self-esteem. Self-respect. The sense of your own value or worth as a person.

In short, your self worth is simply your opinion of yourself or the value you place on yourself. Some individuals have high self-worth. They are sure of who they are and the value they possess. Others have yet to realize their worth due to any number of circumstances.

<><><><><>

49

"A diamond in the rough may not know its true value, yet it is still valuable."

For the most part, most people have a pretty good idea of whether or not their self-worth, self-esteem, or their self-love is high or not. There are even situations where a person's self-worth varies depending on their environment and their circumstances. Your self-worth can be very high in your workplace but be very low with your family.

Low self-worth is a very noticeable trait with most individuals. There are a few ways to recognize if your self-worth is low. Often, you expect negative things to happen to you. You expect to be discarded and rejected. If you have low self-worth you are mostly not very comfortable in social environments. This is not simply because you are shy. This is usually because you are afraid that others already have a negative opinion about you. You may even be the life of the party. However, in this case, it is not because you thrive in that role, it is because you need to have someone pay you a compliment. You seek validation from others because internally you believe that you are not worthy.

For the most part, having low self-worth keeps most individuals seeking beauty and happiness. Your life is not truly your own because you are not quite sure if you are valuable enough to even be noticed, so you try very hard to be.

There are some of you who, when you get into a certain place in life, are more likely to remain in that position opposed to allowing change to take place. You are also more likely to claim certain emotional issues, problems, and even physical issues. You are sure that there is something not quite right with you and that you are not worthy of having a good life. Due to some mental, emotional or physical abuse that you have suffered or some physical differences, handicaps or "defects", you have such a low self-perception.

Those with low self-worth tend to see life from a fearful state of mind. In this state, it is easier for someone else to have control of your entire life. You are sure that they know best and you often see them as more valuable then you, so the things they have to say are almost law to you.

< >< >< >< >< >

"The saying, 'Life has many ups and downs,' does not have to include your self-worth."

As I mentioned before, there are those who experience both highs and lows in their self-worth. Whereas those with low self-worth tend to be in that state most of the time, those with self-worth ups and downs tend to vary in their perception of themselves on an almost regular basis. At work they are very confident in themselves. They believe that they are an asset to their company or their business. However, upon getting home everything is different. They are no longer as confident of their value.

51

This is Conditional Self-worth. This is also what I call "up and down" self-worth. Conditional self-worth is based on how good things are going at the time. It is based on what a person has done or accomplished, how much money they have made, or what they are able to contribute. These thoughts come from the belief that if things in their life are good then it must mean that they are doing something right. When these things are not so favorable, their self-worth is then low.

When circumstances, conditions or your assets determine how good you feel about yourself, these things control you and your life. Thus, you can never be completely content.

Examples of Conditional or "up and down" self-worth would be when a person falls into a deep depression and gets down on himself because of the loss of a job or significant other. Or, when a person blames himself for everything and says things like, "I can't ever do anything right." Conditional self-worth is evident when a person is very happy because their sales at work are at all-time high, but commits suicide when things are tough.

Understand that there are times when we all get down on ourselves for something we thought we could have done better. The thing is not to let that feeling remain a player in the game.

<><><><><>

> *"Self-worth comes from one thing -*
> *thinking that you are worthy."*
> *-Dr. Wayne Dyer**

Dr. Wayne Dyer is the author of *Your Erroneous Zone*, *Excuses Begone* and also *The Shift: Taking your life from ambition to meaning*. When I found the above quote, I wanted to know more about the person who said it. I researched and found that Dr. Dyer had been born into a dysfunctional family filled with abuse and poverty. As a result he ended up living in various orphanages.

The kind of situations Dr. Dyer faced are often what leads to low or zero self-worth and low self-love. When your environment is negative it is very easy to buy into the idea that you are not valuable enough to have anything good in life.

There are many who have experienced these things in life. But people such as Dr. Dyer, Spiritual Life Coach and author Iyanla Vanzant, and Motivational Speech Coach and author Les Brown, are just a few examples of individuals that have come from unfavorable beginnings yet rose to lives that are all their own. They are now teaching and encouraging others to believe in themselves and to push forward with the valuable things they possess on the inside.

If you have high self-worth you are more of a go- getter,

you are more likely to take personal responsibility for the changes and the choices that you make in your life, and you are more likely to step out and do something big, just because you believe that you can. You believe in yourself.

This high level of self-worth gives you the root of your positive attitude and a positive attitude is what is needed to accomplish great things in your life.

<><><><><>

"It's now your responsibility to take charge of your self-concept and your beliefs."
- Jack Canfield*

There is not a thing wrong with you! You are worthy of a great life. Learning to love and respect yourself is most important at this time in your life. This is where you begin to truly understand your value in this world. Getting to know who you are and what you have to offer is vital to the success of anything you set out to do.

We are going from low self-worth, conditional self-worth and varying self-worth to high and unconditional self-worth. It is time to get over "I'm not worthy." You are worthy. You must believe this!

The honest truth is that I can tell you this one hundred times. You can pay your money to your life coach, a therapist, to buy book after book, or to attend every em-

54

powerment seminar that comes near you. However, if you are not ready to do what it takes to replace that old thinking and belief system, you are going to continue with your low and/or up and down self-worth. It is your responsibility to take the next step. I believe that you are ready. So, "Let's 'GO'!"

Time To 'GO'!

You are now going to learn more about yourself by following the next three steps.

- Find time for yourself. This step will help you to clear away the chatter in your mind so that you can simply listen for your inner voice or The Higher Power that resides on the inside. Some ways to do this are to simply have complete quiet when you are riding in your car, or wait until everyone in your house is asleep, or actually take a trip to a place that can allow you the seclusion that you need. This time is vital because this is the time when you will meditate or pray for clarity.

- Journal your thoughts and then reread them to see where you are coming down on yourself too hard. This will help you to begin to see a pattern that needs changing. You are not a mistake. You do have great value. Now it is time for you to realize these facts.

- Write down your likes, your needs, your desires, and your beliefs. When you begin to write down the things about yourself that you know, this will allow you the time to actually remember that you too are a great and unique individual.

Likes:

_____
_____
_____
_____
_____
_____
_____
_____
_____
_____
_____
_____
_____

Needs:

_____
_____
_____
_____
_____
_____
_____
_____
_____
_____
_____
_____
_____
_____

Desires:

_____
_____
_____
_____
_____
_____
_____
_____
_____
_____
_____
_____

Beliefs:

_____
_____
_____
_____
_____
_____
_____
_____
_____
_____
_____
_____

Get Over That Fear

<><><><><><>

"I have heard fear defined as an acronym: 'False Expectations Appearing Real.' We are often victimized more by the false expectations than by the reality." - Les Brown*

Often times we look at fear as simply a part of life. Though we are all born with a certain level of cautiousness or what some may call a natural fear which protects us, I believe that the fear we are going to discuss in this chapter needs to be defined.

Fear is defined as *a distressing emotion aroused by impending danger, evil, pain, etc. whether the threat is real or imagined; the feeling or condition of being afraid*. This is one of the definitions given by Dictionary.com. However, the definition I want to focus on are, *concern or anxiety*, and *that which causes a feeling of being afraid; that of which a person is afraid*.

To be afraid of means *to be full of fear of. To be filled with apprehension, to be filled with feelings of reluctance, unwillingness, distaste, etc.*

The kind of fear that I want to discuss is the kind of fear that has us crippled and paralyzed when there is, almost always, no a reason to be.

Most people are likely to fear things that are in no way a threat to their lives. We allow our fears to cause great crippling in our lives. Because we fear the outcome of a certain situation, we tend not to embark on any challenge. Therefore, not much gets done in our lives. Not many goals are reached. We are afraid of taking a step toward what we want.

We all know what it means to be crippled. Yes, there are adults who are crippled physically and may need certain accommodations to accomplish a goal. But, if they are not crippled in their minds they are still able to reach those goals. Facing a particular fear; not allowing it to stagnate you, is being courageous.

<><><><><>

"If you don't make it your business to overcome fear, you better believe it will try to overcome you."-Judith Orloff, MD*

We often become slaves to our fears. When we have become imprisoned to those fears, crippled by those fears, this is the point where we can say that being afraid has now overcome us. The natural cautiousness, mentioned above, is one thing, but being bound by fear is something completely different.

The fear I am talking about goes far beyond the basic fight or flight instinct. There is the fear of failure, the fear of rejection, the fear of losing, the fear of speaking in public, the fear of loving, the fear of trusting, and there is even a fear of success.

These are examples of the fears that cause us to live our life on permanent pause. This is not the way life should be lived.

<> <> <> <> <>

"Unlearn fear! It's possible!"

There are occasions when fear seems to be a part of a person's very nature, like when every little pain makes them nervous and afraid. However, often fear is learned. We learn to fear from the media, via the news or some information on broadcast. We have learned fears which we adopted from our parents and grandparents. We learn fear from our abusers. We learn fear from watching other people's experiences. We even learn *it* from our favorite cousin. The one that doesn't even know the facts of the situation, but always has a negative thought or reaction.

"Don't jump down the stairs, you might break your neck and die." Now you have a fear that if you do what you were just told not to do, you might actually lose your life.

Whether we know it or not, we learn fear from some of the smallest things that are implanted in our minds from childhood to adulthood.

For the most part, fear is learned so we must unlearn it. *"There is nothing to fear but fear itself."* This is a quote from a speech given by President Franklin D. Roosevelt. What does this statement mean however? What would make this statement hold substance? Maybe, it is the fact that fear in itself causes, at times, crazy and ill-considered actions. Being fearful, we either act before thinking or we don't act at all which may still cause a horrible outcome.

If you have a fear of failure you will, most likely, not even try. The fact is, you can be the best at this particular thing but without trying you will never know because you cannot even muster the courage to proceed.

If you have a fear of rejection, as I used to, you may not want to send letters for grants or apply for that high position because you are afraid you won't be chosen. Then again, you will never know unless you go for it. There are a lot of feelings of "I missed out," just flying around in the air.

If you have a fear of trusting, it is probably due to something you have experienced or what you have witnessed by watching others. Your mother trusted someone and she got scammed. Your sister believed the story that turned out to be a lie. However, not every situation ends with the same results. But honestly , there is no way that we would ever find out if we are too afraid to give it a try.

One of the things that I find most funny is that when there is a 3 in 2000 chance for a negative result, a great many people will focus on the 3 instead of seeing the whopping 1997. Go figure. We can't see the positive results in our face for looking at the negative ones.

<><><><><>

"The odds of succeeding at being a great You are favorable. Look on the positive side of the number line and you will never notice the negative."

I want to urge you to begin to look closer at the 1997 chance that is positive. Or, focus on whatever side the positive result is on, even if it was the three. Why? Because, there *is* a chance of a positive result just like there is a possibility that something else could occur. But, honestly, who wants to spend their whole lives just "knowing" that something is going to go wrong?

Begin today by taking an intentional look in the direction of the positive result. Not every ant bites. Not every person will let you down in love. It will not always be the other person to get the job. Your ideas will not always be overlooked. However, we must remember that life is life. Things will happen that are not favorable.

In some cases, another person may be more qualified. Another idea may be more suitable for the situation. Have you ever stopped to think that just as you want a favorable outcome, others may be hoping for one as well? So, don't be afraid to step out sometimes. If you don't try you will never know what could happen.

Furthermore, when the situation does not turn out the way you want it to, remember that this is not always a bad thing. Sometimes it did not work out because all your attention needs to be focused on the great thing that lies ahead of you.

Time To 'GO'!

This activity will require you to use resources such as your Internet, your local library, or your local bookstores.

Go online and in your search box enter the words "quotes on overcoming fear" or "affirmations of overcoming fear". This should bring you to a page that lists a great number of websites that offer quotes and/or affirmations on the subject.

After you have searched you are to take a pen and write down at the least 21 quotes on the subject. Why the number 21? Because it is said that 21 days of doing something creates a new habit.

Take one quote a day and repeat it to yourself over and over again until it is ingrained in your memory and planted in your soul. These will be quotes that you decided to use, so the new thoughts will be those that you believe will help you live a more positive, confident and fearless life.

Throughout your day when you are tested with a negative feeling or negative thought I want you to remember your quote and repeat it to yourself over and over again. Do this in your mind if you are at work and say it out loud if you are alone. Also, while you are online, search with the words, "books on self confidence" or "books on overcoming fear". You can be specific on the type of fear that controls you.

After your search results are up, look through your options and choose two books. This is where your local library, bookstores or online stores come in to play. (*Also take a look at the resources in the back of this book for some ideas.*) These books will be for you to feed yourself with more positive thoughts; thoughts of courage that will help you create more self assuring habits.

Write down your quotes here:

1.

_____
_____
_____
_____
_____

2.

_____
_____
_____
_____
_____

3.

_____
_____
_____
_____
_____

<u>4.</u>

_____
_____
_____
_____
_____

<u>5.</u>

_____
_____
_____
_____
_____

<u>6.</u>

_____
_____
_____
_____
_____

<u>7.</u>

_____
_____
_____
_____
_____

<u>8.</u>

_____
_____
_____
_____

9.

10.

11.

12.

13.

_____
_____
_____

__14.__
_____
_____
_____
_____
_____

__15.__
_____
_____
_____
_____
_____

__16.__
_____
_____
_____
_____
_____

__17.__
_____
_____
_____
_____
_____

18.

_____

_____

_____

_____

_____

19.

_____

_____

_____

_____

_____

20.

_____

_____

_____

_____

_____

21.

_____

_____

_____

_____

_____

Let's 'GO'!

Write your book choices here:

<u>1.</u>

_____
_____
_____
_____
_____

<u>2.</u>

_____
_____
_____
_____
_____

Use this space to write down any extra you may find.

_____
_____
_____
_____
_____
_____
_____
_____
_____
_____
_____
_____

<u>Get Over The Past</u>

<><><><><>

"The past is made up of things that can no longer hurt you."

I know that most people get tired of hearing others tell them to get over their past. It is hard to fathom, from the receivers viewpoint, how anyone could honestly expect you to get over a time in your life that has literally changed the way you live and see life.

More often than not, these words are spoken to those of us that carry around so much baggage that we are not even able to stand up straight, if at all. "Get over your past" is not just advice that is meant to hurt your feelings or brush off your pain; it is meant to help you to become free.

This chapter is for the hurt, torn, abused, victimized, sad, frustrated and angry. This is for you, the one who is still holding grudges from the 1800's. This is for the big-hearted person that feels all used up; the one that thinks they will never be able to give of themselves again.

73

It's time to get over the past and live for the moment.

<><><><><>

"Stop acting as if life is a rehearsal. Live this day as if it were your last. The past is over and gone. The future is not guaranteed."
- Dr. Wayne Dyer

There are a few things that I know. I know that the second that has just passed in my life will not be returning. I also know that I am not promised the second after this one. Why is knowing these things so important to me? Because they help me to evaluate what is worth dwelling on and what is not. I have come to learn that I cannot dwell on any one thing. Even when I am making a good memory I have to continue to let the time flow. I cannot pause at one second and stay there.

Yes, I am aware that the things you went through were tragic; very horrific. I am not making light of your emotions concerning the situation. What I am saying is that though it was terrible then, the act that was taking place is now done and over with. You are still allowing it to hold you as if it were happening at this very moment. That cannot be true because at this very moment you are reading this book.

It does not profit you to hold on to those things; those hurts. It only helps you to keep up the walls of steel.

74

These are the walls that you will not allow anyone to penetrate.

Due to your past filled with hurt and suffering, you are now in a place where if you do not let it go you will be the one causing the pain. Those who you love, or the ones who love you, will be the ones who suffer the most. Hurt people who are still clinging to the pain of the past tend to become the abuser.

The memory of your negative past is like that bully who used to hold the back of your shirt in school. The more you try to get away, the stronger the grip became. It is time to break free of that hold.

<><><><><>

"It is not the pleasures of the past that keeps a person stuck, it is the comfort."

For some people, the past is the greatest place of comfort. No matter how bad it was, they were or are comfortable because the place is familiar to them. After being abused, torn down, manipulated and controlled for so long, the word "freedom" to your bound up state of mind feels a bit scary. The situation may not be ideal, but at least you know what to expect. There are no surprises.

I have heard story after story about women and men in abusive relationships who are no longer staying because of love or care. They remain there because they feel that if they were to break free, they would not know how to function. They are afraid that they won't be able to live without their abuser. This is their comfort zone. They had the comfort of routine and though the situation is not good for them, they would rather remain in a place that is familiar.

The comfort of the situation, the routine of it all keeps them in a place where bad things will continue to happen. When these persons are finally to the point where they *can* break free, they are so tied by what has happened in their past that it often takes years to truly become free.

It is possible to get over your past no matter what the circumstance has been. It is possible to find a new comfort zone, one that will be full of peace and total life fulfillment.

<><><><><>

"You cannot deny your past happened because it would be a lie. However, you can let the past remain where it is. It has happened. It is over. It is done."

It will be pointless to pretend as if the past did not happen. It was in the past that we were all conceived. You were mistreated in the past. You were abused in the past. You were talked about in the past. You were touched in the past. You were called names in the past. You were belittled in the past. You were abandoned in the past. Yet, you are here to live on. You are here to go forward.

When I was young, I was teased for a number of reasons. My hair was too long, so they pulled it. My nose was too big for their liking, so they laughed at me. They teased me about being adopted because my mother was light skinned and I was brown. Though I wasn't really adopted, the teasing used to get to me. I cried very often because no one seemed to like me.

After so many years of teasing and bullying, I started to grow tough skin. I did not like being teased so I decided that I wouldn't take it anymore. I developed an attitude and was determined that I would not let anyone treat me badly again. I carried that attitude with me for a very long time. I was mean!

It hurt, and the older I became the more attitude I developed. However, underneath it all I was a girl who wanted someone, besides my mom and immediate family, to give me some positive attention. So, I sought out the attention from anyone who would give it to me. This pattern stayed with me until one day I became tired of allowing what I did not receive in the past to dictate who I would be for the rest of my life. Now I am determined to live for the day. I am not looking neither do I need anyone to validate me. I have been valid since my creation.

What I began to discover was that I deserve to be happy *now*. I want you to carry that same message with you. It is *now* that is important. *Now* is when you are living. *Now* is when things are better. *Now* is when you have a new opportunity to live with a peace of mind and to do this in *your* freedom.

<><><><><>

"Whatever your past has been, you have a spotless future."
– Melanie Gustafson

It is time to get over your past! It is time to stand up and say, "I am no longer a slave to shame, guilt, abuse, victimization or fear!" "Let's 'GO'!"

Time To 'GO'!

Not everyone can admit that the past still holds them hostage. Here are a few question to be answered that can tell you the truth once and for all. Are you still holding onto the past?

Is there anyone from your past that has hurt you in any way that you have not yet forgiven?

_____
_____
_____

Are you afraid to trust another person with your heart because of a failed relationship?

_____
_____
_____

Is it hard for you to think about the past? Do you still cry about something that happened long ago?

_____
_____
_____

Are you still holding on to grudges from someone stepping on your shoe 20 years ago?

_____

_____

_____

Are you still angry with your family for how they treated you when you were young? When was the last time that you spoke to them?

_____

_____

_____

If any of these questions sparked something inside of your Being, you may still be living in your past. Evaluate what you have written and research the ways to begin the repair of what is broken on the inside of you. The first step to doing that is knowing that you are ready to get past it all.

Get Over Stubborn Pride

<><><><><>

"Pride goes before destruction, a haughty spirit before a fall."
— *Proverbs 16: 18*

The feeling of being proud is something that we have all experienced. According to Dictionary.com to be proud is a feeling of pleasure or satisfaction over something regarded as highly honorable or creditable to oneself. It is having or showing self-respect or self-esteem.

We have felt this upon completion of a very important goal. It has been felt while our children are performing in some way. We have experienced being proud when our names are spoken in the same sentence with any mention of high honor.

Pride in the sense of feeling pleasure and satisfaction is very common. It is okay to feel this sense of pride. However, when *simple* pride turns into *stubborn* pride, it is time to re-access ourselves.

Stubborn means having or showing dogged determination not to change one's attitude or position on something, especially in spite of good arguments or reasons to do so.

Stubborn pride is that pride that will not allow you to forgive, that will not let you compromise with the people you love. It will not allow you to yield to your Creator. You have it your mind and heart that you will not bend to change or reason. It is this level of pride that has caused many people to lose their jobs, homes and families.

This pride does not like to admit when it is wrong, even when knowing what the truth and the facts are. It will not allow you to take food when you know you are hungry, water when you are thirsty or help when you truly need it. This level of pride is destructive to you.

<><><><><>

"My pride, my stubborn pride, had me blinded."

I understand that circumstances have happened in life that have caused you a serious need for caution. There has been one too many occasions where a person has misused you. Or, each time you have asked for help, you have been rejected or the favor that someone has done for you has been thrown back into your face.

I was at a point, once upon a time, when I decided that I

would not accept anything from anybody. I wasn't asking either. I kept saying, "God will take care of me." Well, needless to say, though God was taking care of me, I kept missing the provision that was being sent. Every time I turned someone's help away, I was missing it.

I was so clever. I thought that I was protecting myself and my feelings. In actuality, I was blocking myself from any opportunity or blessing that was to be sent my way. How blind was I?... How blind are you?

<><><><><>

"A proud man is always looking down on things and people; and, of course, as long as you're looking down, you can't see something that's above you."
- C.S. Lewis

There are many people who deal in stubborn pride on a daily basis. It is often so bad that others don't care to be around them. Most people choose not to keep company with someone who never apologizes for being rude because they don't see why they have to. Is that you?

When you have stubborn pride, you tend to look down on anyone who chooses not to see things your way. You believe that you are too good for those who do not have as much as you have or who have not accomplished all that you have accomplished.

If you are carrying that stubborn pride with you, now is the time to let it go. Of course, you first have to admit that you have it. You will probably say, "I'm not like that, I just know when I'm right and I need them to understand that I'm right as well." You will see things your way and fold your arms at this chapter and try to look over it.

Well, if you are not sure if this is you, let's do a check list. If you have said any of the following things, you may have stubborn pride.

- I don't need any handouts. I can do this myself.
- I'm not wrong about this one. You'll see what I mean later on.
- He should have never did that to me. I forgive him but I am never going to forget.
- Well, if she decides to leave then that is on her. I won't apologize because I didn't do anything wrong.
- I will never shop there. Who wears that cheap stuff anyway.

Are you on the list?

<><><><><>

"I will not allow any level of pride to keep me from my blessings. I want it too badly to let it be taken by my stubbornness."

84

Is not apologizing worth losing your friendship or any relationship? Are your feelings of pleasure and satisfaction so much that you are bordering on arrogance? Is stubborn pride worth starving to maintain? Are you so unyielding that no one can convince you to change your mind when it's made up, even for a good cause? Does your pride cause you to see yourself as better than rather than equal to another?

Though it is okay to take pride in your accomplishments or the success of those you love, it is an entirely separate state of pride that causes our destruction. It is time to realize where you sit on the pride meter and if you need to find a way to relax it. "Let's 'GO'!"

Time To 'GO'!

What is the difference between simple pride and stubborn pride?

_____
_____
_____
_____
_____
_____
_____
_____

If you are filled with stubborn pride, answer the questions posed to you in the chapter, then write down what you can do to overcoming this level of pride.

_____
_____
_____
_____
_____
_____
_____
_____
_____
_____
_____

Get Over Yourself

<><><><><>

"The hardest things to get over sometimes is yourself!"

There are a few different situations where the phrase "get over yourself" is used. I did not realize this when I first decided to write this chapter. Now, I am amazed at the number of ways it can be used just depending on the context in which the statement was made.

According to urbandictionary.com, the phrase is used to tell someone that you believe they hold too high an opinion of themselves, or are behaving in a conceited or pompous manner.

In that context, the phrase would be something that I would say to a person who is very arrogant. One who thinks so highly of themselves that they begin to down or belittle someone else for the sake of making themselves look better. This is the context in which I had always used the phrase.

Dealing with people who have such huge egos that they honestly believe that others are beneath them can really make for a bad day at the office. There is nothing wrong with loving our liking yourself. You should always be confident and sure, however, not at the expense of someone else to the point of making them doubt themselves.

So, to the arrogant I say, " get over yourself." Life is not only about you. It is about having enough confidence in yourself to realize that you are vital and very important to the plan of this world. We are working with others that bring their own, unique something to the table. We need each other. You're not better than anyone else, just unique.

<><><><><>

"I know that it's your party, but why are you crying again?"

Jennifer Beckham, in her book, *Get Over Yourself: 7 Principles to Get Over Your Self and On With Your Destiny* says, "God actually put it this way to me. 'It's time to get over yourself!' A bit harsh? Maybe. But what I couldn't understand was that I was the one standing in the way of God's plan for my life. He wanted me to get over my own self issues..." Though this message was spoken to Jennifer I believe that it carries a lot of weight.

We often fall on hard times, and just as often we don't always want to get up when we fall down. We would prefer to stay in a rut and cry, day in and day out. We often ask for help, but just as often we don't hear the voice when it is answering telling us to get up, be joyful and keep moving. Your little "woe is me" party is saying woe to your progression.

You cannot move forward with your joyful and peaceful existence if you are miserable, dwelling and speaking, all the time, of the things that make you feel that way. There is no one issue in this world that belongs to only you. There are other people that have experienced hard times and pain. You are not alone.

During my pregnancy in 2007, I had my own "woe is me" party going on. I was living with some shame for being pregnant again outside of wedlock, mostly because of my religious convictions at the time. What I learned from my years growing up was that it was better to marry than to continue having children outside of marriage and be labeled as promiscuous.

I struggled with myself and my worthiness. I was so depressed that I did not even want to look into the eyes of the three children I was already raising. I loved them. However, I was not emotionally stable enough to be the mother that I needed to be.

I shut myself off from everyone. The only reason why my mother saw me was because she had a key to my apartment. She dropped by often because she was worried and I was not giving her a reason *not* to worry. She wanted to send me to a hospital – a mental hospital - because I was just not coming around.

One day, a friend of mine got tired of watching me slip away. She called in the troops. My mentor and a few other people decided to give me a reality check. Did I want to hear it at this time? No, not particularly. However, I needed to hear it all. I needed that real voice to help me snap out of my tiny little "woe is me" party.

After a few small powwow's with those who cared, I was able to at least get out of my bed. I was able to pray again, for I had stopped doing that as well. I decided from that moment on that I had to snap out of it simply for the sake of living. I wanted to live.

<><><><><>

"Get off the floor kicking and screaming. Use that energy to try something new - to keep dreaming and pushing forward."

How do you react when you do not get your way? Are you upset whenever you cannot have things the way you want them all the time?

In this case "get over yourself" means that you should try to understand that you can not always kick and scream for what you want. This is when you say to the spoiled acting that life is not centered around you getting your way all the time. "By any means necessary" is not our way of doing things. If you do not get the results you want the first time, remain humble yet confident and try, try again.

There are times when not hearing the response you want to hear really gets to you. You want things to go your way so you need to cry, complain, fuss or manipulate. This is not healthy. Not hearing the response that you want to hear does not mean that it is the end of the world, so why pitch a fit!

This is something that we do in our relationships. We tend to be so caught up in what will please us, that we fail to remember that a relationship is give and give, not give me, give me, give me!

<><><><><>

"Focusing on a greater cause often helps you take the focus off the negative circumstances in your life. Focusing on someone who has a greater need often takes your mind off of what you do not have."

It is very easy to focus on all of the negative around you. Looking at the negative makes it hard to see the positive; the silver lining. Even with the confidence that you should build up within yourself, we are still here together to live out plans for our lives. If we focus on the greater cause, we will have less time to insult others. There will be less time to stay locked away up in your "woe is Me" party. It will also make it difficult for you to have time to kick and scream about what's not right in your life.

Change your focus so that you can be a master of getting over yourself. "Let's 'GO'!"

Time To 'GO'

Take a week and focus your attention on someone else. Be careful to avoid arrogance and feelings of superiority toward others.

Pick a different thing everyday that will cause you to hear and understand another person's plight. Then, help in whatever way you can. At the end of each day, write down what you felt and also how the recipient reacted to your gestures. After this week is complete, try another week.

Day One

_____
_____
_____
_____
_____
_____
_____

Day Two

_____
_____
_____
_____
_____
_____
_____

Day Three

_____
_____
_____
_____
_____
_____

Day Four

_____
_____
_____
_____
_____
_____

Day Five

_____
_____
_____
_____
_____
_____

Day Six

_____
_____
_____
_____

_____

_____

Day Seven

_____

_____

_____

_____

_____

_____

Let's
Get On!

Get On With Finding Your Purpose

<><><><><><>

"... From a very young age, it was obvious that I was born to sell."
- Tana Goertz*

We were all born with something special that we can offer the world. This is my belief. It does not matter how small that something may seem, there is still value in it. For some, knowing your purpose was as automatic as breathing. You knew exactly what you wanted to do and what your purpose was long before some people even realize what they liked.

I want you to be confident that you are full of purpose. In my book, *PurposeFull You: You Are Full of Great Purpose,* I wrote that there is great purpose in all that we see someone else do. Whether it be the local store clerk, the camera person taping the news anchor, the assistant cutting the fabric, the nurse cleaning the wounds of the patient or the chauffeur getting the employer to their meet-

99

ings or appointments on time; it is all purposeful. Find your purpose   and   remain at the highest point of confidence. Your purpose is no less great than anyone else.

I love to say that without the camera person the news anchor can never be seen. Without the mail carrier our important documents would never get to us. Without mascots, teams would just not be the same. Everyone plays a vital role.

<>< >< >< >< >

"The first step to knowing your great purpose is to start getting to know you!" *

What makes you unique? What sets you apart? This "being" is not something that someone else has to see. It could be something that you keep hidden from the world because you are afraid that they may think it shallow. That doesn't matter because this is what makes you unique.

What are your talents and gifts? What brings a great burst of joy and peace to your spirit every time you do it? It could be something as simple as helping children feel comfortable with themselves. You could have a great gift of communicating. There is something that you can bring to the table that makes everyone stand up and notice.

There are three things that I suggest as you begin to know yourself in order to know your purpose. Begin your day with meditation, make a list, and remind, research, relax.

First, begin to take time every day to pray and or meditate. In this time you can ask for guidance, make it known that you want to know your purpose and be still in order to begin reflection on what brings you joy and peace. This has become one of my most favorite times of the day.

Second, make the list of your likes, desires, passions and skills. It doesn't matter whether those skills are natural or learned skills. This will help you to get better acquainted with yourself. Writing these things down will bring forth ideas and get your mind moving. The things that really click with you will most likely give you an unexpected boost of "Go Get 'Em"! Every time something new comes to you, simply add it to your list. Soon you will realize how enjoyable life can be when you simply allow yourself to be yourself.

Lastly, I want you to remind, research and relax.

Remind yourself , on a daily basis, that you are full of great purpose. Speak the words out loud. "I am full of great purpose." "I am more than capable of fulfilling the task ahead." Speak positively to yourself constantly. No one else is responsible for you remaining positive. We are simply here to help cheer you on.

Research those that inspire you. Ask yourself if what inspires you the most about this person is something that you can most closely relate to. Would you like to do something similar to what this person does? Would you like to model them? Only *model* them, because you are a great, unique individual with your own capabilities that will be added to make that purpose your own.

Relax in the fact that only you can do what you do the way that you do it!

Time To 'GO'!

What positive things do you need to remind yourself of?

_____

_____

_____

_____

_____

_____

_____

_____

_____

_____

_____

What person or persons inspire and influence you the most? What about them remind you of yourself?

_____

_____

_____

_____

_____

_____

_____

_____

_____

_____

What are your desires and your passions?

_____
_____
_____
_____
_____
_____
_____
_____
_____
_____
_____

If you had to answer on the spot, what would you say that you believed you were born to do?

_____
_____
_____
_____
_____
_____
_____
_____
_____
_____
_____

Get On With Living Your Life

<><><><><>

"You must accept complete responsibility for your choices and decisions, and for everything that happens as a result of them, from this day forward."- Brian Tracy*

In the book, *The Power Of The Platform: Speakers on Success*, Brian Tracy says, "The mark of the mature person is his or her level of 'response - ability.'" This is the ability to respond with positivity in life's situations. Whether it be personal or business, a mature person has learned to have a positive outlook on life.

I believe that it is important to remember that everything in life is cause and effect. If you make a decision, make sure that you have weighed out everything that may occur so that no matter what the effect, you were already aware before the fact. It is very important that we know and understand this lesson in life. With this in mind we will always take responsibility for our own actions.

One of the things we had to learn in our earlier years was responsibility. Not everyone had this lesson but a great number of us did. A part of that lesson for me was not doing whatever it was that I wanted to do, and then praying that the outcome would turn out in my favor. There is always the voice inside of you that lets you know when you should turn around and walk away from something. This is not to keep you from doing what you like, it is to help keep you from those unfavorable outcomes.

While you are getting on with living your life, remember to trust that will inside of you, as long as it is not screaming for you to do something that would disrespect or harm another. It's time to live your life. It's time to move forward.

<><><><><>

"The reason it does not make sense is because it's not supposed to."

Not everything is supposed to make sense. Be sure that you do not cause yourself any undue stress by trying to make sense out of everything that life brings. The logical answer will not always be the right answer for your situation.

Following your instincts and not your fear will more often lead to a better outcome. During those times when you know that you are afraid be sure to pay attention to the chatter in your head. This is not simply your intuition kicking in. This is an actual battle between your faith and your fear. When this happens, breathe deep and allow yourself time to relax. Then, get ready to step out. Be courageous, because you never know what lies ahead of you. If you try to make sense of everything, or you allow your fear to make decisions for you, you will never go far.

<><><><><>

"Be true to and honest with yourself. It is you that has to be around you even when the lights go out and no one else is around."

Evaluate what you believe on a regular basis. If you've been taught a particular thing but it does not ring true to you, then you are not being true to yourself if you have to force it. You are not living in faith when it comes to that teaching. Faith cannot be forced.

You can be yourself and still live in harmony with others. Respect is a very important factor. We all want it, but most of us are not practiced in giving it. Let each individual be who they are and not what you think they should be.

Know that who you are is good enough, but never stop growing. You cannot stand the rest of your life trying to measure up to an ideal. You are who you were created to be. Be proud of that and never lose sight of the fact that you are a unique individual with much to offer.

Develop your craft. Consider wisdom. Gain as much knowledge as you can and don't forget understanding. Be true to who you are and you will find peace around every corner.

<><><><><><>

"Every time I make an effort toward my dream, another door opens."
- Angelique Daniels*

It is time for you to live your dream. Find where you fit, where you want to be, and began walking towards it. Just walk out. You have what it takes. Do not ever believe that you will not have what you need to do what you need to do. For everything that you are intended to do, you will be equipped for the job.

Choose the career or business that you want. What have you longed to do or experience, but have held back because it wasn't the right time on the right season? It is time to dream again. Not just dream it but go get it!

Be sure to choose your path because it makes you happy and complete. One mistake that many people make is that they choose the path of their lives based on the finan-cial aspect. There is nothing wrong with the financial side of things, however, it is a fact that finances alone do not bring fulfillment. We are here to live this life not simply exist in this world.

<><><><><>

"You must love and allow yourself to be loved in the process. Life without love is merely existence."

Another way that you are going to get on with living your life is by allowing yourself to be free to love.

The word love has been so overused and misused that it seems to have lost its effect. Yet, real love still exists and I know that you want it. Honestly speaking, even the person who claims that they could care less about love wants it. Love helps us grow. It builds us up. There is nothing like having love as you embark on your journey.

I know that there are those who have been scarred and who have vowed to never love again. You are strong and determined. You are sure that you will not need anyone else in your corner to fulfill your dreams. I do not deny the fact that you could do great things. You can achieve anything you want to, whether you have someone else there with you or not. Yet, having love in your life gives you an extra boost of energy and adrenaline.

We've already talked about getting over, now we are getting on with life. A part of what you got over was the past.

The hurt and pain from those times are done. Do not allow anything from that time to subject you to a life alone. Love is worth it.

<><><><><>

"Keep yourself fed! Motivation is the food of choice."

Always have materials in your possession that will uplift you, motivate you and speak to you. You have to feed yourself with positive things or else all the negative you see will over take you. (See resources)

The same way our daily food intake nourishes us, so does being fed by books, positive speeches or spiritual teachings. We have to keep ourselves geared up to be able to face any challenge. When you are daily encouraging yourself or allowing someone else to encourage you, you are already two steps ahead of the game.

Now is your time to start living. Now is your time to get over so that you can get on with life. "Let's 'GO'!"

Time To 'GO'!

How do you intend to start living your life? What have you always wanted to do?

What will you use to keep yourself motivated throughout the week? What do you need to do in order to keep it up?

_____

_____

_____

_____

_____

_____

_____

_____

_____

_____

_____

_____

_____

_____

_____

_____

_____

_____

_____

_____

_____

_____

_____

_____

_____

_____

Let's 'GO'!

Close your eyes and picture your ideal life. What does it look like? (Remember that it is possible.)

_____

_____

_____

_____

_____

_____

_____

_____

_____

_____

_____

_____

_____

_____

_____

_____

_____

_____

_____

_____

_____

_____

_____

_____

_____

Bonus Get Overs

Get Over Total Selfishness

To be selfish means to be devoted to or caring only for oneself; concerned primarily with one's own interest, benefits, welfare, etc. regardless of others. It is concern or care only for oneself.

Just like pride, there is a certain level of selfishness that is healthy for us as humans. Without this small amount, we would neglect to take care of ourselves. A great many of us carry the weight of being many things to many people. Mom, dad, mate, child, sibling, employee, employer, friend, confidant, counselor, coach, mentor and so much more. We wear many hats. No wonder we tend to lose our sense of self in the shuffle. So, it is only fair that we take out some much needed time to care for ourselves.

That means that sometimes we have to turn off the phone, we have to meditate and pray, we have to take long hot showers or baths, we have to treat ourselves to pampering. It even means, sometimes, saying no to extra task. Selfishness in this way can be very healthy for you.

What we are trying to avoid, however, is the cut-throat mentality in the world today that says that every one must be out for themselves or there won't be enough to go around. It has become so that people have stop helping others out of fear that another person will steal their spotlight.

It has become a trend to look out for self and self alone. This trend is pointless and needs to be abolished. Sacrifice is a great part of life. "Let's 'GO'!"

Time To 'GO'!

What platform do you have that may be of benefit to another that is trying to find their way?

_____
_____
_____
_____
_____
_____
_____
_____
_____
_____

What can you do, this month, to show that you are not totally selfish and that you understand our need for each other in this world?

_____
_____
_____
_____
_____
_____
_____
_____
_____
_____

Take action this week. Give someone a surprise helping hand. Write down how they felt and what you felt in doing this. Has it inspired you to do more? If so, what did it inspire you to do?

_____
_____
_____
_____
_____
_____
_____
_____
_____
_____
_____
_____
_____
_____
_____
_____
_____
_____
_____
_____
_____
_____
_____
_____
_____
_____

Get Over That Judgmental Attitude

We were all born to be individuals. As a world we have so many different nationalities, cultures, races and religious practices. Everyone brings something different to this great, big world.

Why is it acceptable for you to like what you like, believe what you believe and practice what you practice, yet it is such a terrible thing for someone else to have their own convictions?

Does any one person have the right to force what they believe to be true on another person?

Regardless of what a person chooses to believe or practice, there are areas where we can all relate to one another. There are universal principles and teachings that encompass us all. We have our differences, yet those differences do not give us room to judge another.

Most times, it is the way we were brought up that causes us to have a judgmental attitude toward others. We are taught that "our" way is right and someone else is wrong. But, I challenge you to see things with different eyes. "Let's 'GO'!"

121

Time To 'GO'!

Write down how you feel when a person with a different view point or belief tries to force you to believe what they believe.

_____
_____
_____
_____
_____
_____
_____
_____
_____
_____

How important is it that others respect your position on any given subject?

_____
_____
_____
_____
_____
_____
_____
_____
_____
_____

Can faith be forced?

_____

_____

_____

Challenge: Sit down at least once in the next week and determine the similarities between you and someone that you may consider to be "wrong" in their way of doing things. Write them down.

_____

_____

_____

_____

_____

_____

_____

_____

_____

_____

_____

_____

_____

How can you show that you have respect for these people without trying to get them to change their beliefs?

_____

_____

_____

_____

_____

Write down three things you can do to change a judgmental attitude.

1. _____
_____
_____
_____
_____

2. _____
_____
_____
_____
_____

3. _____
_____
_____
_____
_____

Let's 'GO'!

7 Day
Journal

Use this journal space to write down
your thoughts for 7 days.
Then at the end, document what
has changed in your life.

Day 1

Today I...

_____

_____

_____

_____

_____

_____

_____

_____

_____

_____

_____

_____

_____

_____

_____

_____

_____

_____

_____

_____

_____

_____

_____

_____

_____

_____

_____

_____

Day 2

Today I...

Day 3

<u>Today I...</u>

Day 4

Today I...

_____

_____

_____

_____

_____

_____

_____

_____

_____

_____

_____

_____

_____

_____

_____

_____

_____

_____

_____

_____

_____

_____

_____

_____

_____

_____

_____

_____

Day 5

Today I...

_____

_____

_____

_____

_____

_____

_____

_____

_____

_____

_____

_____

_____

_____

_____

_____

_____

_____

_____

_____

_____

_____

_____

_____

_____

_____

_____

_____

_____

Day 6

<u>Today I...</u>

_____
_____
_____
_____
_____
_____
_____
_____
_____
_____
_____
_____
_____
_____
_____
_____
_____
_____
_____
_____
_____
_____
_____
_____
_____
_____
_____

Day 7

<u>Today I...</u>

_____

_____

_____

_____

_____

_____

_____

_____

_____

_____

_____

_____

_____

_____

_____

_____

_____

_____

_____

_____

_____

_____

_____

_____

_____

_____

_____

_____

<u>Sources</u>

1. Willie Jolley – from *It Only Takes A Minute To Change Your Life!*

2. Willie Jolley – from *It Only Takes A Minute To Change Your Life!*

3. Brian Tracy – taken from *The Power of The Platform: Speakers on Success*

4. Les Brown – taken from *The Power of The Platform: Speakers on Success*

5. Shalonda "Treasure" Williams – taken from *PurposeFull You: You Are Full Of Great Purpose*

6. Dr. Wayne Dyer – author of *The Shift: Taking Your Life From Ambition To Meaning*

7. Jack Canfield – taken from *The Power of The Platform: Speakers on Success*

8. Les Brown – taken from his book, *Live Your Dreams*

9. Judith Orloff, MD – author of *Emotional Freedom: Liberate Yourself From Negative Emotions and Transform Your Life*

10. Tana Goertz – taken from *The Power of The Platform: Speakers on Success*

11. Shalonda "Treasure"Williams – taken from *PurposeFull You: You Are Full Of Great Purpose*

12. Brian Tracy – taken from *The Power of The Platform: Speakers on Success*

13. Angelique Daniels – taken from *The Power of The Platform: Speakers on Success*

Resources

1. *One Day My Soul Just Opened Up* by Iyanla Vanzant (For spiritual feeding)
2. *It's Not Over Until You Win* by Les Brown
3. *Get Over Yourself: How To Drop The Drama and Claim the Life You Deserve* by Tonya Pinkins
4. *Get Over Yourself: 7 Principles to Get Over Your Self and On With Your Destiny* by Jennifer Beckham
5. *The Day Begins With Christ* by Adrienna Turner (For spiritual feeding)
6. *TruSum's Excerpts To Exodus* by Tru Sum (For spiritual feeding)
7. *The Power of Now* by Eckhart Tolle (For spiritual feeding)
8. *Epigphany: A Health and Fitness Spiritual Awakening* by Angelique Daniels
9. *The Chicken Soup for the Soul* ® series originated by Jack Canfield
10. *Self-Esteem: A Proven Program Of Cognitive Techniques For Assessing, Improving, and Maintaining Your Self-Esteem* by Matthew McKay and Patrick Fanning
11. *Five Steps To Overcoming Fear and Self Doubt* by Wyatt Webb
12. *Fearless: Imagine Your Life Without Fear* by Max Lucado

From The Author

Thank you so very much for taking the time to read this book. I do hope that you were able to take something form it that will help to empower you.

I would love to hear from you. Please email at treasuresyw@lovewalkmotivationservices.com.

Visit me today at
www.treasurespeaker.co.cc or
www.lwmotivations.co.cc.

Peace,
Shalonda "Treasure" Williams

P.S.- There are times when we all need a boost. It is okay to admit that we need help getting on track. If you are at that point, please don't hesitate to contact me for your free 30 consultation today. 641-715-3800 code: 15994

Coming Soon

New From Shalonda "Treasure" Williams

Let's 'GO'!:
Your Personal Motivational Journal

Also, Other books by the author include:

Love Walk Meditations: Back To The Basics

A Heart's Thoughts: Love Walk Meditations Series

PurposeFull You: You Are You Full Of Great Purpose

Look Out For:

Motivating Yourself In Just 21 Days

Becoming P.R.O. Self: Get Back To Knowing, Loving and Honoring Self

Made in the USA
Columbia, SC
20 December 2017